The Story of Mount Batten, Plymouth

Arthur L. Clamp

*The changing use of this small area of land
overlooking Plymouth Sound
from a Stone Age Settlement to its present use
as a R.A.F. Station.*

The most well remembered aspect of R.A.F. Mount Batten — the famous seaplanes.

This version of the book is virtually as originally published.
There are now additional pages at the back providing information about the author.

The republishing project is being managed by Arthur's grandson, Steven Gibson. We aim to find all the research that he was involved in publishing, preserving it for the next generation as part of 'The Clamp Collection'.

Introduction

The story of Mount Batten is a very complex one covering 2,000 or more years of use from the time when it was probably a small fishing and agricultural settlement to its present use as a R.A.F. Station where equipment and systems of communications include many computer aids often associated with larger enterprises.

The preparation and research for this booklet has not been without some difficulty especially for the early uses of this headland and for the pre-war years of the Station. Records and photographs are almost always being made or taken but few appear to survive either in a good condition or accessible in a local library. The two World Wars brought much change and activity to Plymouth but also a considerable amount of devastation not only to buildings and streets, etc., but to the once extensive records and newspaper files upon which a study like this so heavily depends.

However, it has been possible to piece together the varied story of the Mount Batten peninsula from local and national records and from people who have served at the Station and from some who are still there. Its appearance today belies the very interesting and varied number of events that have taken place on this small piece of land which was once quite accessible to local people. The most well known years of its story were when it was used as a seaplane base when planes could be seen taking off or alighting on the sea close to Mount Batten and when the Station itself was open to the public, mainly during the inter-war years, when thousands of people spent a day looking at the then large and interesting seaplanes otherwise viewed from a distance or in the air. The seaplane base was very much part of Plymouth and its planes were perhaps the most evident of the many military associations that the city has had for many years with the three services.

Although the Station for the past decade or so cannot match the exhilarating days of the last war with the comings and goings of troops, planes and equipment, it is still performing an important role but in a less apparent manner. The meteorological work work undertaken has grown in extent and importance and the Station's position in the South-West still gives it a key role to play in the surveillance of the seas many miles away from land.

I must place on record my many thanks for the co-operation I have received from R.A.F. Mount Batten through the Station Commander who was here when much of preparatory work was being undertaken, Wg. Cdr. J. E. F. Williams. Special thanks must go to Mr. Terence Hugo, who is employed in the catering section of the Station. He has taken a great interest in the history of Mount Batten and was able to supply photographs and sources of information. Lastly the staff of the West Devon Library and many other people throughout the West Country must be included in these thanks for their help.

The Early Settlers at Mount Batten

One of the surprising things about this small peninsula of land, now covered with modern buildings and workshops, is that from all the evidence discovered here it appears reasonably certain that this was the first locality to be occupied by early man in the Plymouth area. For about the last 150 years a large number of artefacts, stones, coins and the remains of animal bones have come to light during the many building schemes undertaken here and this, to date, points to Mount Batten being occupied at least 2,000 years earlier than Plymouth!

One of the earliest finds was a Stone Age polished stone axe dating about 2,500 B.C. and, from tests made on it, was proved to have come from Westmorland where a Neolithic axe-making site was then in use. It has been deduced that the headland was the most likely site of the settlement and the high ground, where Fort Stamford is, was part of the site of an early burial ground. A Bronze Age ring has also come to light dating from about 1,200 B.C. this being a common ornament to wear on the arm during that period. The settlement of people here may well have been partially dependent for food on the sea as many shells have been turned over, among these being the remains of oysters, whelks and limpets together with bones of deer, dogs and pigs. It was also during this period that Dartmoor was occupied by tribes who first came across the sea from France penetrating the lowland forests of Devon by following up various rivers, one being the Plym. Is there any connection between this movement of people and the settlement at Mount Batten?

There is quite firm evidence that by about 800 B.C., the later years of the Bronze Age, a permanent and thriving settlement was in being here. Bronze axes including one of a type associated with Brittany, gouges, chisels, knives and sickle blades all indicate that a variety of activities were taking place from trading over the sea to cultivation of land. Fragments of bronze cauldrons, made of sheets riveted together, and quantities of scrap bronze metal further indicate that some form of metalwork had also taken place involving smelting. Many bronze implements, including mirrors, were uncovered during the digging of the foundations for Fort Stamford found, in most cases, in graves numbering between three and four hundred. This was a very large number of burials for the period and gives a good indication of the size and importance of the settlement in this area.

The occupation of the site during the Iron Age has been confirmed by many relics being unearthed dating from these years. In 1832 gold and silver Iron Age coins came to light in a quarry and elaborate bronze work, bracelets and pins for fastening clothing can also be identified with this period. A thick layer of rubbish or refuse seems to have built up over much of the area which further shows an extensive and long occupation of the site. Contemporary with the metal finds came a wide variety of pottery remains, earthenware and some glass.

The later inhabitants of this area continued living here until at least Roman times as personal items such as brooches, rings and bracelets were then being made in period styles and many coins of the old empire, some suggesting trading with other countries, have added further evidence of long occupation. The people used Roman coins and these cover the reins of Emperor Nero (A.D. 54-68) to the Emperor Gratian (A.D. 367-383). This was by now quite a large settlement and appears to have been the only one with firm indications of either trading with the Romans in the Plymouth area or being involved with their occupation of England. The nearest main outpost of their empire was at Exeter so it could be that Mount Batten was a staging or beacon station of some kind for this south-west corner of Devon. Other items uncovered from this period are pieces of pottery and a potsherd with the letters *LMANQ* scratched on and, at nearby Hooe Lake, a statuette of Mercury, the patron saint of merchants, was found. In all this must have been a very active settlement and certainly the largest of its kind in the area.

Coins and artefacts found on the Mount Batten site.

With the departure of the Romans from this country during the fifth century A.D., little evidence has yet come to light to point to Mount Batten continuing as a large settlement. The fact that no relics have yet been uncovered does not necessarily mean that the encampment closed when the Romans left. In all probability the site was occupied for many more years and the folk depended to a greater degree on local trading and resorted to a life style of small farmers and fishermen.

It is known that the land was under cultivation during the 1200's by which time the early encampment had gone and the area had come into the possession of one of the local landed families. From this period the peninsula was known as *Howe Stert* or high place with a headland, a name that stood until the years of the Civil War, when it changed to its present title.

The very few records of these years that refer to this locality, tell of problems over silting caused by land disturbance on the moorland by tin miners and the silt being taken down by the river Plym and deposited in the estuary. It was also during this period that Cattedown and Sutton Harbour became the main berthing areas for the large fleets of Elizabethan ships, made famous by the exploits of Sir Francis Drake and Sir John Hawkins. It is fairly certain that Howe Stert would have been used in one way or another in connection with this maritime activity possibly for beaching craft for cleaning and repair work. The peak of this development came during the latter part of the 1500's.

The Civil War Fighting and the Tower

The next definite reference to Howe Stert was in connection with one of the plagues which occurred in Plymouth during the 1620's. The headland was used as a pest house and victims were ferried over from the Barbican and left to look after themselves. A great many died and were buried on the spot and remains of bones disturbed during building work over the past fifty years or more could well have come from this dreadful outbreak. There have been others who have been buried here as well. The numerous shipwrecks along this rocky coast often resulted in mariner's losing their lives and they would have been interred in the nearest soft ground and, no doubt, some of the bones that have come to light originate from these unfortunate sailors. Lastly, Mount Batten was a French prisoner-of-war camp for a time and many soldiers perished here.

Another early record tells of the narrow neck of land between the headland and the mainland, where Fort Stamford was built in the 1860's, being partly breached by the sea. There were great fears over this as, had this been allowed to remain, the peninsula itself may well have become an island at a later date. However, an order was issued by the town authorities to barge owners using the estuary that rubble and refuse was to be dumped in the breach and this eventually filled in much of the opening. A wall was then constructed to hold in the rubble and eventually the land regained its permanence. One interesting result of this dumping from the old town is that clay pipes, pottery, etc., has often been disturbed and the area may be worth investigating properly by archaeologists.

An artist's impression of a Civil War scene in Plymouth.

Perhaps the most important event to have taken place at Mount Batten prior to its use as an R.A.F. Station was its involvement in the battles of the Civil War during the 1640's. Plymouth stood out for the Parliamentarian cause and was successful in withstanding a siege by Royalist troops until their cause failed and Cromwell became head of the nation. The old town, defended by walls and outworks, was the only place to have successfully withheld the advance of Royalist troops in the South-West. Various high points around the town were fortified or earthworks were built up on the main approaches to the town, one being from the direction of Plymstock down to Mount Batten from where an attack across the water could have taken place. The landward side of Plymouth was well fortified but the seaward approach was open to sudden attack if the Royalists could get in close to the shore. Earthbanks were built at Mount Batten and on the higher ground, known then as Mount Stamford, with parallel ditches affording some degree of shelter.

Although much of the fiercest fighting between the sieged troops and the Royalists, under the command of Grenville, took place on the northern flank of the old town there were quite strong skirmishes at Mount Batten because of its closeness to the heart of the town and its harbour. There was one regiment of about 300 foot soldiers and a troop of horse quartered at Plymstock whose duty area covered the headland and it was learnt that an attack on Mount Stamford and Howe Street was imminent. This was in October, 1643. It is recorded that about 300 men were ferried over to Mount Batten from the Barbican and, at dawn the following day, attacked and surprised the enemy guarding this approach. A Captain Slowly, one ensign and fifty-two soldiers were captured while two colours and three barrels of powder came into the hands of the Parliamentarians.

Meanwhile Dartmouth had fallen to the Royalists which freed more soldiers for duty around Plymouth and, by the 21st October, 1643, there were sufficient troops assembled at Plymstock to plan a campaign at capturing Mount Stamford and Mount Batten from which point guns could be fired over the water into Plymouth. During the night of the 21st they dug semi-circular earth banks on the high ground from which defensive position an attack on the lower slopes of Mount Batten could be made. However, the defenders were not to be thwarted. The next day a three hour battle ensued, the Royalists were repulsed from their newly dug positions and one captain and fifty prisoners were taken. A guard of thirty soldiers and one ensign was placed there during the next night but the ensign quitted his position when the enemy was approaching so by the following day the high ground was, once again, in Royalists' hands. The ensign was shot for his cowardice. This position was of such importance in the eyes of the siege troops that the Royalists had to be cleared from the high ground overlooking Mount Batten at all costs and so a lengthy battle ensued resulting, once again, in the Royalists retreating. The costs to the Plymouth troops were high. A Captain Corbet was shot in the head, three other Captains were wounded, some twenty men were killed and about 100 were wounded. The Royalists lost a few men but they were able to retreat out of shot towards Plymstock, the Plymouth men had to stand their ground as they were cut off from the town by the sea.

This state of affairs continued until 5th November, 1643, when the Royalists brought into close position guns and opened up with 200 demi-cannon and whole culverin shot breaking the defending line towards the Oreston flank. During the night the breaches were partly filled with woolsacks but without avail. The attack was renewed the following morning and by about noon the Plymouth troops were running out of ammunition and provisions were exhausted by eight days of engagement. They signalled to the town for help but this was not forthcoming, so they had no choice but to agree to surrender terms. Out of the 300 who were ferried over to Mount Batten some thirty-six were still at their positions. At 4 p.m. the Captain surrendered marching out with flying colours, matches lighted, and carrying bag and baggage. So Mount Stamford fell leaving the smaller Mount Batten open to attack.

An earthwork had been prepared here at the commencement of the fighting and some of the Plymouth troops had retreated to it in the hope that they would be relieved from the town before hostilities broke out at this lower level. However, their hopes were in vain. The Royalists marched down to Mount Batten and after a short battle the weary troops from the sieged town were overcome by much larger numbers and they, in turn, surrendered so giving up the headland to the Royalists who now had the command of the estuary and were in a position to fire cannon into the Barbican and the defences built on the Hoe (the Royal Citadel was not built until after the Civil War).

A report drawn up two months later after this loss stated that although the town was frequently under attack from batteries positioned on Mount Batten no one had been killed but buildings suffered damage and one vane of the windmill on the Hoe had been hit and fell off! Fortunately for the besieged people of the town and the war-weary troops the Royalist cause failed through events in other parts of the country (the Battle of Naseby) and so the siege was raised and the surrounding high land occupied by the enemy cleared. It was from this period that Mount Batten took its name. Until these years it was known as *Howe Stert*. It had come under the command of a certain Captain Batten, afterwards promoted to Admiral Batten, who was designated Governor of the headland and the tower.

The Restoration of the Monarchy in 1660, the crowning of Charles II, brought a reversal of fortune for Plymouth, the town that had so valiantly withstood the Royalist's attacks. Charles II ordered the building of the Royal Citadel on the Hoe which was constructed during the 1660's and the tower at Mount Batten which is still standing on the limestone headland. This move was partly to increase the defences of Plymouth and partly for the King to maintain a close watch on the erstwhile rebellious citizens. Mount Batten tower, known for many years as Mount Batten Castle after which one of the inns was named, was fortified with cannon for guarding the entrance into the then main harbour area (it was not until the 1690's that the Docks at Devonport were started). The tower has recently been restored and equipped with cannon from the Tower of London. It is protected as an ancient monument and is open to the public by appointment through the Station.

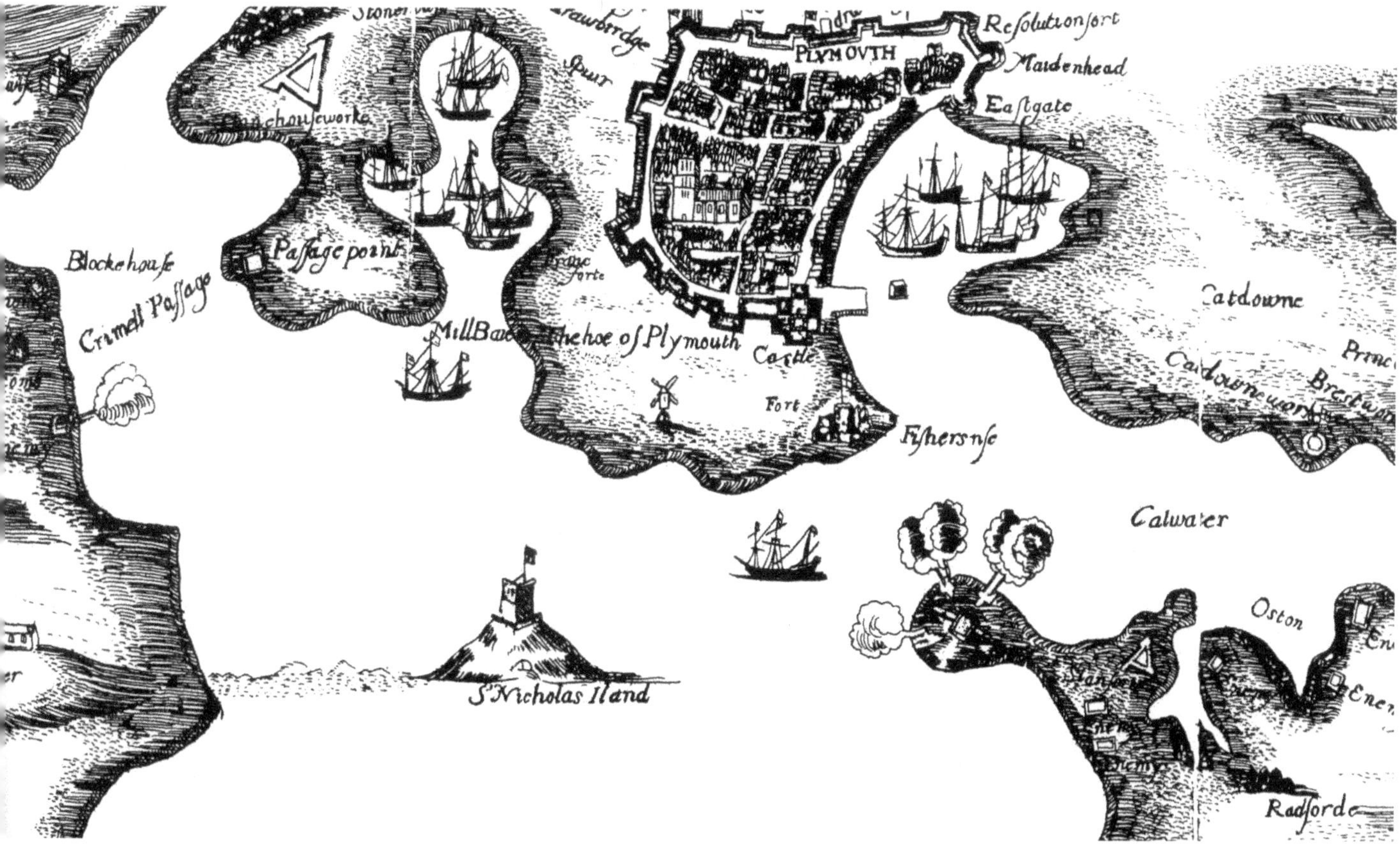

Mount Batten's old defensive castle or tower built in the 1660's.

Mount Batten from 1800 to 1913

These years were relatively quiet ones for Mount Batten when only the call of the sea birds could be heard above the breakers on its rocky shores and then later the cries and laughter of people enjoying themselves during the time it was used as a fairground and holiday area for the town dwellers of Plymouth.

Although there was a great deal of shipping activity along both shores of the estuary during the last century, including quite substantial ship building work at Turnchapel, Mount Batten was mainly left to itself and a few hard working quarrymen seeking to make a living by cutting limestone for burning from the headland and cliff towards Turnchapel. In 1839 a licence was also given by John, Earl of Morley, the landowner living at Saltram House, for prospecting for iron ore and, in that year, some 56 tons were shipped to a smelting works in South Wales. However, the quality was so poor that by 1841 the smelters refused to accept it so this small enterprise soon came to a prompt end. A further but unsuccessful attempt was made to work the Wheal Morley iron mine in the 1870's.

On the seaward face of the peninsula a row of coastguard cottages were built during this century. Smuggling had been a problem for many years along much of the Devon coastline and steps had been taken to maintain a careful watch along it. The coast was divided into sections and each had men keeping a vigilant eye over the coming and going of boats. The coastguards were also very valuable in times of extreme weather when ships were often wrecked (see article) and assistance was close at hand to the mariners in trouble.

In the 1860's Fort Stamford, overlooking Mount Batten, was constructed as one of a ring of large forts encircling Plymouth because of fears that Napoleon would be invading England. Much of the limestone rock used in the building was taken from the headland which later endangered the tower standing above the station. This old round defence tower had long been put to other uses, one being a look-out for the coastguards who also used it as a signal station. This was a fairly common practice around the coast and church towers or any other tall building would be put to a similar use. Flags were hoisted and messages would be transmitted over short distances, in this case over the water to either the Royal Citadel or to the Barbican.

The largest undertaking during these on the peninsula was the building of the breakwater in 1881. Its purpose was twofold. In spite of the much larger breakwater affording shelter to boats in the Sound, the actual harbour area in the estuary was often difficult to navigate in stormy weather. There was also the continuing problem of erosion on the headland associated with the much longer silting of the entrance channel. In 1874 the Cattewater Harbour Commissioners were formed under whose guidance the breakwater was built. It is a little over 900 feet in length and follows the line of the well-known Mount Batten reef whose rocks had brought tragedy to many of the old sailing ships. It has been put to a variety of uses from affording local fishermen with a good vantage point over deep water to the years when planes were lowered or raised from the water and carried along by means of metal rails running its length.

The building at its head was the *Breakwater Inn*, presumably erected at the same time, which became the second inn to serve the needs of visitors and locals prior to Mount Batten becoming an R.A.F. Station. The other house was the *Castle Inn*, a much older establishment, taking its name from the tower, then known as the castle. This catered for the thirsty needs of the coastguards, fishermen and others engaged in various maritime activities on this side of the estuary. This inn was demolished in the 1960's to make way for the R.A.F. sergeants' mess, and it was the second building to bear this name, the first was in the form of a tower.

Perhaps the most popular use Mount Batten has ever had was during the years preceding 1913 when it was used as a holiday haunt for Plymothians and, on public holidays, as a fairground to which boats ferried over hundreds of people for one penny a crossing. This undeveloped area of land, with its small beach and headland close to the town, provided a welcome break from the crowded streets of old Plymouth which could be reached within minutes at little expense.

On public holidays it became very popular, with a fairground going full blast, supported with cockle stalls and all the usual side shows and entertainments eagerly looked forward to by generations not accustomed to long holidays. The two inns did a brisk business with the visitors; a pontoon stage made landing quite easy and the headland itself gave excellent views over the Sound. In all this small area of land must have been Plymouth's nearest thing to a resort where the older citizens recall people sunbathing, swimming or just walking around on most summers' days.

An early engraving, c1830, showing the tower and open headland.

Shipwrecks around the Peninsula

This small peninsula of land forming part of the eastern shoreline of Plymouth Sound situated at the entrance to the Laira estuary has had more than its fair share of shipwrecks ever since records have been kept. The reasons will become apparent if a map of the South West is studied and the prevailing wind direction is kept in mind. The old sailing ships were completely dependent on wind for their movements and as these varied and changed from one direction to another or very stormy conditions occurred, so the chances of making for safe harbour or anchorage diminished according to the severity of the weather.

The prevailing wind is south west blowing up the channel and bringing ships into the Sound with ease when conditions were good. However, if conditions were bad, and they frequently were during winter months, ships were often blown on to the eastern shore of the Sound or torn from their anchors only to be dashed upon the nearest rocks.

These adverse conditions and the fact that the Cattewater was the main harbour, made the old sailing craft particularly vulnerable to the Mount Batten peninsula. Conditions did improve a little with the construction of the main breakwater (1812-25) and the breakwater from the peninsula itself in the 1880's but these two improvements were more than counteracted by the increase in the volume of

Two sailing ships aground by Mount Batten in 1872.

shipping using the Sound during the last century, which resulted in an overall increase in shipwrecks. It has only been during the last fifty years or so that any substantial reduction in the number of ships floundering has taken place, mainly through the use of radio communications, better weather forecasting, etc. so today a wreck is something of an unusual occurrence and when it does take place there are often reasons other than weather which cause it.

One of the earliest records of ships running aground at Mount Batten was in 1362, when a severe storm wrecked a number of them around the Sound. There must have been many before this time as the old port was under constant attack from pirates and from the French coast. In 1287 some 325 ships were assembled at Plymouth for an attack across the Channel and no doubt, quite a large number of attacking boats would come right into the Laira estuary on revenge incursions.

A winter gale of 1689 resulted in HMS *Centurion*, carrying fifty guns, being wrecked on Mount Batten along with the *Henrietta* of sixty-six guns. These were large ships for the time, the first of 513 tons. The reef running out from the headland was so dangerous that between 1712 and 1716 old ships were deliberately sunk on it in an attempt to form a small breakwater. These were the thirty-six gun prize vessel *Saudadoes*, HMS *Dunwich* and HMS *Moor* and, much later, the larger HMS *Vengeance*, all old ships from the Navy.

The 1790's continued in the same vein as the previous hundred years with shipwrecks marring the mariner's calendar with almost unfailing regularity. The major wreck of these years was the East Indiaman *Dutton*. The ship was sailing for the West Indies with part of the Queen's 2nd Regiment aboard when bad weather forced the captain into Plymouth on 26th January, 1796. She struck Mount Batten reef and then was swept helplessly onto the rocks below the Hoe. Some 600 men were rescued under the direction of Sir Edward Pellow. The closing years of this period were marked with two further wrecks off the small peninsula. First the schooner *Ebenezer*, laden with culm, went ashore in 1798 and then two months later the frigate *Pallas*, of thirty-two guns, grounded in the same place. One crew member died as huge seas swept over the ship.

More accurate records were now being logged of shipping accidents and wrecks showing that numbers were increasing almost every decade. This situation eventually led to the building of the main breakwater in Plymouth Sound and the smaller breakwater from Mount Batten itself. The great gales of 1797, 1803 and 1812 left an indelible trail of broken ships around the Sound and strengthened the arguments for the construction of the main breakwater.

There was heavy loss of life when HMS *Amethyst* was wrecked on Mount Batten in 1811. She was driven from her anchorage in a south west gale and hit the rocks just after midnight. One account of this tragedy gave the figure of 600 as having drowned during the night. Numerous skeletons have come to light from time to time during excavation and building on the peninsula and it could be that some of these came from this wreck or others here? The storm of 1817 resulted in three vessels being wrecked on this rocky shoreline and at Bear's head, on the far side of the Hoe. At Mount Batten, the brig o'war, HMS *Jasper*, with sixty-seven people aboard came to grief with the loss of all but two souls. The list of wrecks at this point is almost endless. The *Haydon* and the *Espoir* went ashore in 1828. Others followed in 1861, 1865, 1868, seven wrecks in 1872 and so on until the closing years of this century. The pattern was consistently one of ships being driven ashore mainly during the winter storms or occasionally by navigational errors when ships were crossing the Sound.

Although the overall number of shipwrecks around the Sound started to fall during the opening years of this century, winter storms still resulted in the loss of ships and life. In the Christmas hurricane of 1912 five ships went aground, one being the Brazilian river steamer *Goyaz* on Mount Batten rocks. She was not seriously damaged and was later able to get off on a high tide.

A New Role for Mount Batten from 1913

The year 1913 was a turning point for Mount Batten which partly juts out into the Sound and situated in such a position that its new role was to play a vital part in the First and Second World Wars. A flying base was established on the headland on 2nd September, 1913, but it was another three years before its potential was fully realised as a base for flying boats to patrol the Western Approaches. By 1916 the German Navy had deployed submarines over a large area of sea which was causing considerable anxiety since one of the most vulnerable areas affecting this country was the Western seaboard. At this period most of the Naval Air Stations were located on the east and south-east coasts and it became vital that similar stations be developed along the west coast and Irish Channel if the submarine menace was to be effectively met.

Mount Batten provided an excellent site for an Air Station from which air patrols could be mounted and sustained over the entrance to the English Channel and the eastern areas of the Atlantic. The Sound, protected as it is by the Breakwater part way across its entrance, provided a suitable take-off and alighting area, and the presence of other Naval Units in Plymouth was also an important factor in deciding to develop this site.

An old photograph of seaplanes on the Station pier.

HMS Rapid ferrying personnel R.N.A.S. Cattewater.

Urgent steps had to be taken in setting up the Air Station as by now the First World War was continuing longer than first anticipated and the German Navy was gaining considerable experience in handling the new submarines year by year. Towards the end of 1916 plans had been prepared and in February 1917, the land was requisitioned from its owner and the Station established as *R.N.A.S. Cattewater*. The initials stood for the Royal Naval Air Service, this branch of the services being originally engaged in developing the plane as a fighting weapon. The coastguards officers and few civilians living on the headland were obliged to leave and the old Castle Inn became the residence of the first Station Commander, Wg. Cdt. S. W. Smith, O.B.E. It was renamed *Greenleaf House*. So the new and dramatic role which Mount Batten was about to undertake started. Plymouth extended its military sphere by now taking in a branch of what was shortly to become the third and newest service of this country. She had long standing connections with Naval and Army Units and now she was about to welcome the Royal Air Force within her boundaries.

Work was soon put in hand by the demolition of the old civilian houses and in their place were constructed huts to accommodate service personnel and equipment. These were in use until 1938 when they were then replaced by the present Airmen's Mess and the three-storied permanent barrack accommodation block. Four hangars were erected, three of which are still in use. One was destroyed during the last war and its site is now occupied by the Station Supply Squadron. Metal rails were laid along the length of the Breakwater for a travelling crane which was used to hoist the seaplanes into and out of the water. Within twelve months the new station was ready to receive its first seaplanes which for thirty years or so were to become a common sight over the Sound and from which many historic flights either started or finished. Little did the pioneers of this station think of the vital role their aircraft would be playing during the difficult years of the Second World War.

By the beginning of 1918 there were five flights of *Curtis* seaplanes at Cattewater, Nos 347, 420, 421, 422 and 423. The main task of these was escort duties with Naval craft, particularly with destroyers, and anti-submarine and reconnaissance patrols. One

The recommissioning ceremony in 1918 at the Station.

R.A.F. Cattewater, 1918 to 1928

unexpected feature which marked these early years was the drafting in of the largest company of the Women's Royal Naval Service (W.R.N.S.) in the South-West, no doubt bringing to the new station added interest and debate over what had been considered men's responsibilities. Mount Batten was still quite difficult to reach by land so the customary boat or ferry, now named HMS *Rapid*, continued to carry personnel between the Breakwater and the Barbican.

...ors eagerly awaiting to view a seaplane during a Station open day.

On the 1st April, 1918, following the recommendations of the Smut's Report, the Royal Naval Air Service and the Royal Flying Corps were merged to form the Royal Air Force and from that date RNAS *Cattewater* became R.A.F. *Cattewater*. An impressive ceremony was held in front of any Breakwater House (formerly the Breakwater Inn), the white Ensign was lowered and the flag of the Royal Air Force raised in its place. With a change in title to the Station came changes to the structure of the various flights and the planes used. The first seaplanes were replaced by the more efficient and powerful *Short 240 Flying Boats* and the *Short 184 Seaplanes*. To these were later added *Sopwith Baby Seaplanes* and *Felixstowe F5 Flying Boats*. No doubt many flying personnel of the last few years would be astonished to fly under the same conditions and with the same machines as the pioneers did from Mount Batten. The planes looked so frail and small when seen from the Hoe either taking off or coming to alight on the water under the Royal Citadel. They were so light that it was possible to raise them out of the water by a small crane working from the Breakwater. One incident is recorded from these early years about the hazards of flying over water in these planes. Two airmen were making a flight over the Scillies when they had to ditch due to engine failure. The seaplane overturned on hitting the water and the two men had to endure three days in the water clinging to the plane's floats before being picked up.

During 1918 the Station came under the control of No. 19 Group, South-West area: it then became part of the Coastal Defence Forces. Two flights were added during this year, nos. 348 and 349, to the existing five flights and these were formed into two Squadrons (Marine Operations). In spite of these changes, the ending of the war brought about necessary disbandments which took place a year later on 15th May. Within a few months of this date Mount Batten reduced its strength and range of activities. The German menace had passed, shipping lanes were clear of lurking submarines and Mount Batten had discharged its duties most conspicuously and had made a worthy contribution to winning the war in a sphere of fighting not previously experienced.

By 1922 R.A.F. Cattewater disposed of most of its planes, personnel had been drafted to other stations, activity had been cut down to a minimum and the base reverted to a Care and Maintenance level. However, 1923 brought some attention to it with the publication of a Bill entitled the "Cattewater Seaplane Station Bill" giving authority for the outright purchase of Mount Batten. It was stressed by the Under-Secretary of State that no other land was available for use as an enlarged Seaplane Station.

For about five years the Station was maintained by a skeleton staff as there was some uncertainty as to its future. Other sites for development were being considered but by the middle 1920's Mount Batten, through its position in the South-West and proximity to a relatively calm area of sea, was finally selected for the main base for the new and growing sector of seaplane development by the R.A.F.

This decision was to lead to Mount Batten becoming the most important Station for seaplanes and its subsequent growth as a departing point for them to many parts of the world. The coming years gave plenty of opportunities at gaining experience in handling the new seaplanes which was later put to effective use during the Second World War.

This early photograph shows part of No. 203 Squadron during 1928/29.

R.A.F. Mount Batten, 1928 to 1939

It was mainly through the development of the *Sunderland* and *Southampton Flying Boats*, which were considerably larger and more powerful than the planes used during the First World War, that the Station was to have a new lease of life. In late 1928 a decision was taken to re-open *R.A.F. Cattewater* and plans were put in hand for structuring its use with the larger seaplanes then being made. The Station changed its name to *R.A.F. Mount Batten* from 1st October, 1928, a title which it has retained until the present day. Two months later a Coastal Reconnaisance Flight was formed, No. 482, and then, in the opening month of 1929, it became known as No. 203 Flying Boat Squadron. This was the start of a new era for Mount Batten in which it was to play an even greater role in the defence of this country than it had during the conflict of 1914-18.

The first large seaplane to be put into use was the *Supermarine Southampton Flying Boat*, fitted with two Napier Lion engines, followed by the *Blackburn Iris Flying Boat*. The first came under the command of Group Captain Busteed, O.B.E., D.S.C., who had already gained fame as the pioneer of ship-deck landings. He was the first officer to land a plane on the deck of a stationary ship and among the first four to accomplish the same achievement on a ship under way. Alongside the larger seaplanes in use were others of smaller design. There was the *Fairey IIID* on floats and a *Wapiti* using 30 ft. floats which, on one occasion, did the loop over Plymouth! No. 203 Squadron, however, saw service at Mount Batten for only a very short time. During 1929 it was transferred for duty in Iraq where it remained until 1939.

A second Squadron was formed in its place, No. 209 Flying Boat Squadron, equipped with *Blackburn Iris Flying Boats* which were in use until 1934 when they were replaced with more powerful *Perth Flying Boats*. These aircraft were fitted with three 825 h.p. Buzzard engines which greatly increased the range over which reconnaissance patrols took place. On 1st May, 1935, this Squadron was transferred from Mount Batten to Felixstowe.

It was during these years that Mount Batten held an annual open Empire Air Day when spectators saw a variety of flying displays, seaplanes in their hangars were open to inspection and the personnel on the

One of the smaller planes once in use here.

station generally laid on entertainments and refreshments for thousands of Plymothians and service friends many of whom made this an annual visit. The day was a public relations exercise and many local people still cherish memories of being taken on the ferry to the peninsula for a day's outing and entertainment. The last of these open days finished about 1951.

A third Squadron, No. 204 Flying Boat, was formed at the station on 1st February, 1929, and remained for many more years than the two previous ones. It was transferred in April, 1940, to make way for the arrival of Australian personnel who saw active service here during the Second World War. No. 204 Squadron was first equipped with *Supermarine Southampton Flying Boats*, each powered by two Napier Lion engines, and, on the 31st August of the same year, it was re-equipped with *Scapa Flying Boats* fitted with two Rolls-Royce

Two Supermarine Flying Boats descending to Plymouth.

Kestrel engines. The Squadron achieved fame through a number of exploits during this decade. Firstly, news had leaked out that a certain Aircraftman, T. E. Shaw, was in service at the Station who was better known as *Lawrence of Arabia*. He was at Mount Batten from 2nd February, 1929, to 28th April, 1933, and worked as general orderly for the flight commanders. He was well respected on the station, took his full share of all the normal duties expected of an Aircraftman and was responsible for designing the Squadron's crest. This was based upon a photograph he took of a cormorant with wings outstretched standing on a mooring buoy. The motto of the Squadron is *Praedam Mari Quaero (I seek my prey at Sea)*. He is also remembered for his gallant efforts in diving to reach the wreck of a seaplane in February, 1930, which had crashed in the Sound. Unfortunately his attempts at saving the lives of the crew were not successful.

Many notable flights also started from Mount Batten during this period by various officers and personnel attached to the Squadron. In July, 1930, the longest formation flight for flying boats started from here bound for Iceland and in 1936 another first was chalked up with a flight to Singapore to pioneer a route to the Far East and to test the planes under monsoon conditions. In the following year, five took off for Australia where the Squadron was to take part in the 150th anniversary celebrations of the first landing in that country.

The Squadron's long service at Mount Batten was interrupted for just under a year (1935-36) when it did duty in the Suez Canal Zone taking part in exercises and photographic reconnaissance work. On the return flight two of the flying boats were fired upon by a Spanish destroyer while flying at 3,000 feet over the Straits of Gibraltar. Fortunately only slight damage was sustained by one aircraft.

During the absence of the larger flying boats, others came and made their appearance in the Sound. In May, 1935, No. 407, Fleet Fighter Flight, equipped with *Hawker Ospreys* and No. 444, Fleet Spotter-Reconnaissance, flying *Fairy IIIFs*, arrived from Fleet Air Arm Float Base, Lee-on-Solent. Both remained at Mount Batten until November, 1937, and undertook a variety of duties in connection with the Home Fleet.

A third re-equipping of its planes took place in 1936 shortly after returning to home base. The *Scapa Flying Boats* were superseded by *Saro Londons* which saw service for just three years when they were in turn replaced with the well-known *Short Sunderland Flying Boats*. It was the latter planes which rendered such invaluable service from Mount Batten throughout the Second World War becoming a well recognised sight over the Sound and at their moorings in the Cattewater.

This period in the development of Mount Batten closed with the first encounter of the Squadron in the Second World War. On 18th September, 1939, the SS *Kensington Court* carrying 8,000 tons of grain, was torpedoed about seventy miles from the Scilly Isles. One of the Sunderlands on patrol was ordered to the spot in time for eight of its bombs to be dropped at the point where the U-boat had submerged. The pilot skillfully landed the flying boat and took on fourteen crew while another flying boat from Pembroke Dock rescued the remaining ship's crew. As a consequence of this action the pilot of the seaplane, Flt. Lt. Barrett, received the D.F.C., which was Mount Batten's first of many decorations for gallantry. Although there was a decline in the use of the station during the early 1930's, the later years of this period, marked by the arrival of the *Sunderland* boats, saw a

Another Flying Boat, this time getting ready for take off.

great increase in the level and range of work undertaken. The officers' mess and the permanent accommodation blocks were built and the station as a whole expanded its activities and assumed much of the present day layout. Mount Batten had become by this time one of the most important stations within Coastal Command because of its strategic position close to the Western Approaches to the English Channel which was carrying an increasing volume of shipping.

Aircraftman T. E. Shaw, better known as Lawrence of Arabia.

Marine Craft

Parallel with the use of flying boats at Mount Batten came the R.A.F.'s own fleet of boats which were used to provide a variety of services ranging from refuelling and towing duties to the ferrying of crews and servicing teams to and from aircraft moored on the water. The development of small high-speed craft took place during 1930-31 when trials of these where held, the boats then being known as the *200 Class Seaplane Tenders*. The idea of using these craft was put to the Air Ministry in late 1929 by a Mr. Scott-Payne of the British Power Boat Company who saw a use for this type of craft in the various Flying Boat Stations situated around the country.

Trials of the new boat progressed very satisfactory achieving a speed of 23 knots on one occasion over a measured mile in the Sound. During 1931 additional trials took place with alternative engines and arising out of these came the first of many of the *R.A.F. Marine Craft* used so successfully in conjunction with seaplane bases. One of the crew members during the trials was Aircraftman T. E. Shaw (Lawrence of Arabia) who, co-operating with a Corporal Bradbury, was responsible for writing the original notes on this new class of craft and the famous Air Sea Rescue launches which rescued nearly 14,000 lives during World War II.

The Second World War

At the outbreak of hostilities in September, 1939, the station went on a war footing at once and No. 204 Squadron immediately started carrying out convoy escort duties and search and reconnaissance patrols. These continued until the 1st April, 1940, when the Squadron was transferred to R.A.F. Pembroke Dock and was replaced by No. 10 Squadron of the Royal Australian Air Force. This Squadron operated from Mount Batten for the whole of the war years and had an outstanding record in anti-submarine warfare. It returned to Australia on the 31st October, 1945.

The Australian Squadron was formed on 1st July, 1939, and a detachment was sent to this country to be trained on and then to ferry back *Sunderland Flying Boats* which were required for the coastal defence of that country. It was not anticipated that there would be any undue delay in this programme through the troubles then building up in Europe. However, circumstances determined otherwise and the detachment found itself almost in the front line of battle so that the Australian government placed the Squadron at the disposal of the R.A.F. as part of its contribution towards the war effort. It was the first Dominion Squadron to operate against the enemy and to serve overseas. Thus through a dramatic change in circumstances, not of its own making, this Squadron took the opportunity of throwing itself in with the R.A.F. and discharged this commitment in a most commendable manner.

artime at Mount Batten with a Sunderland just offshore.

Within a month or two of settling in at Mount Batten, and having gained preliminary experience in handling the flying boats, they were fully engaged in escort duties for the dispirited British and French troops being evacuated from France in the face of the German advance. They escorted troop transport ships and naval vessels leaving the French coast and making their way to the safety of the English ports. Plymouth at this time was crowded with thousands of incoming troops and the Sound was full of ships of all shapes and sizes.

The Squadron's first sinking of a German U-boat took place on 17th June, 1940, when one was sighted in the Western Approaches. For this action Sqn. Ldr. C. W. Pearce, then Squadron Commander, was awarded the D.F.C., the first to be gained by the R.A.A.F. Five U-boats were sunk through action by flying boats from Mount Batten during the war. Although this was the most spectacular aspect of their work, other duties included, apart from escort and patrol work, conveying many VIP's from Mount Batten to various theatres of the war and undertaking clandestine missions. The success of the first sinking was marred the following day by the loss of a *Walrus Flying Boat* while on a sortie along the coast of France. A typical exploit of this Squadron is illustrated by what took place on 1st July, 1940. At 0615 hours a message was received at base *Have attacked enemy U-boat-estimate five hits-surfaces-sunk-survivors*. The German commander had scuttled his submarine and there were forty-one survivors waiting to be picked up. Many of the patrols went far out into the Atlantic or down to the Bay of Biscay clocking, on one occasion, 1,400 miles on a thirteen hour trip.

The first of the German air raids to hit the station came on the 15th July, 1940, when a twenty minute raid on Plymouth resulted in four hits on Mount Batten causing damage to the new N.A.A.F.I. canteen, sergeants' mess and one of the slipways. Blast damage was also quite considerable to one of the hangars. On the same day a Sunderland went to the rescue of a merchant ship under attack by five Heinkels in the English Channel, one German plane was damaged and the others made off. A second air raid occurred in the same year on the 28th November when, during a night attack, nearby oil tanks were hit causing an enormous blaze which lasted for five days. A hangar had received a direct hit by a high explosive bomb lighting up the area and so directed more planes to this point. One Sunderland flying boat was ablaze at its moorings and the area within a mile of the station received the brunt of the devastation during this particular raid.

So the war continued into 1941 with the Squadron keeping an ever vigilant eye on the highways of the sea supported by other squadrons operating from Mount Batten. The station had by now become the principal departure point for the Middle East and many important persons passed through, in most cases unbeknown to personnel working here. It also received high ranking officers from Allied countries and personnel from America who landed to be immediately taken to London for important meetings between leaders from both sides of the Atlantic.

Two incidents during this year made news when a Sunderland piloted by Sqn. Ldr. Birch, shot down a Junkers 88, and another flying boat this time under the control of a Sqn. Ldr. Cohen, sank a U-boat with four depth charges. A new role was added to the Squadron when German boats started using French ports, and in particular, Brest. It was necessary to keep a watch and photograph German ship movements which included the *Scharnhorst*, *Gneisenau*, *Prince Eugen* and the more well known *Bismarck*. Some requisitioned civilian flying boats were put on duty at Mount Batten, one of these unfortunately being lost on 19th June, 1941. *Catalina Flying Boats* were by now in use alongside the faithful Sunderlands. The 2nd September, 1941, was

The Australian commemorative wall plaque at the Barbican.

marked by a special 28th anniversary parade taken by Air Vice-Marshall Bromet, C.B.E., D.S.O. at Mount Batten.

In the opening month of 1942 No. 10 R.A.A.F. Squadron returned to Mount Batten from a tour of duty at Pembroke Dock. This redeployment of planes and personnel added to the efficiency of the station much to the cost of the enemy. In July, 1942, a Sunderland from No. 10 Squadron was bombing enemy ships when it was attacked by a fast Me-100 plane which then came under attack from the Sunderland itself bringing it down. The Sunderland, however, was damaged and it was only through the courageous action of two of the crew in throwing out some blazing material that a crash was averted. Two engines were damaged as well but the plane was able to return to base. In August, 1942, a message came in from a Sunderland about to alight on the sea to pick up survivors in a liferaft but, alas, the plane was not heard of again. Presumably conditions were not at their best for this attempted rescue and the Sunderland had crashed on hitting the water. There were occasional difficulties when planes were at their moorings in the Sound especially during stormy weather. On one occasion a ship dragged its anchor and crashed into a Sunderland and, on another, a plane was lost through storm damage even before it had started flying from Mount Batten! A sad note was struck by the loss of life when a plane was forced to land after a mission in which it had sustained damage. Upon hitting the water in Plymouth Sound it crashed killing two airmen and then, when a salvage party was aboard, its depth charges exploded killing nine more personnel.

The year 1943 was notable in U-boat warfare and numerous sightings and attacks were made by the Squadron. Perhaps the most heroic example taken from the records occurred on 1st August when Base was informed of a submarine sighting made by a Flt. Lt. Fry. Flying through heavy defensive fire he pressed home his attack at 50 feet and dropped explosives which broke the back of the submarine. It is thought that the pilots were injured during the attack and died instantly upon their plane hitting the water.

The peak of the German attacks and their submarine patrols had passed and the tide of events was slowly turning in favour of the Allies. Troops and equipment were now being assembled along the coast of Devon and many other places in preparation for the long awaited landings in France. The dispirited troops of 1940 were now in high spirits ready to cross the Channel and clear Europe of the Nazi occupation.

Mount Batten was to play a special role in this undertaking by maintaining a round-the-clock watch on the sea and by the escort of incoming and outgoing vessels to Plymouth. The place was alive with troops, equipment and materials. The station was responsible for weather forecasting for the area, it had an efficient Sea Rescue Marine Unit and a 300 strong Women's Auxiliary Air Force (W.A.A.F.) Unit supporting the Australian Squadron in its work for much of the war. It had by this time also gained considerable experience at handling the *Sunderland Flying Boats* and advised on modifications which resulted in the last model of this plane being supplied known as the *Mount Batten Sunderland*, later classed as the Mark V with twin Wasp engines.

By May, 1944, some 3,177 operational flights had been logged by No. 10 Squadron covering one and a half million nautical miles flown over an area stretching out to the middle of the Atlantic, the Bay of Biscay and Gibraltar in addition to the English Channel and its approaches. The Squadron was awarded its crest by King George VI in 1945, although this was not officially handed over until 1949. With the successful landings on the French coast by Allied Forces the main role of the station ceased. The sea was by now almost clear of enemy ships and submarines and the time was approaching for the Australians to fly from Plymouth Sound for the last time on their homeward journey. On 1st June, 1945, the Squadron was disbanded and on the 31st October, 1945, it left for Australia.

A wartime photograph showing crew and maintenance person

Post-War Developments

The late 1940's saw the end of Mount Batten as a base for seaplanes and brought to a close what were, perhaps, the most exciting and adventurous days the station had seen. The Australians had gone, the developments in flying and other forms of communications rendered the seaplanes obsolete and changes were now well in hand for the station to move into new areas of responsibility in marine operations.

Immediately after the war Mount Batten was transferred from Coastal Command to Maintenance Command and in December, 1945, No. 238 Maintenance Unit was moved to the station. This unit remained until September, 1953, when it was replaced by the Marine Craft Training School from Calshot. In the same year, on the 15th October, the STation Church was dedicated by the Anglican Bishop of Plymouth, the Right Reverend Norman H. Clarke; in the 1960s pastoral services to the station were transferred to St. John's Church, Hooe, after the building was gutted by fire.

In 1961 the Station became the main support base for the Marine Branch of the R.A.F. It is divided into four spheres of activity, these being the *Marine Squadron (Training and Operations), Engineering Squadron (Maintenance Repairs and Overhauls), Administrative Squadron and Supply Squadron.*

Marine Squadron

This squadron performs two of the principal functions of the station, namely, the operating of marine craft and the training of sea-going personnel. It is organised into two flights, *Operations Flight* and *Training Flight*. *Operations Flight* provides marine craft for maritime aircraft operating from R.A.F. St. Mawgan in Cornwall, and to tow targets for the R.N. Gunnery School at H.M.S. Cambridge. It also provides craft to the School of Combat Survival and Rescue during exercises designed to train aircrew in sea-survival techniques and to the Southern Rescue Co-ordination Centre for participation in real or simulated maritime emergencies. A recent development has been the deployment of marine craft off the East coasts of the British Isles to provide towed-target facilities for fighter aircraft operating

ing from patrol, the large steel-hulled Sunderland launch.

HMAFV Spitfire commencing a patrol from the Station.

from bases in East Anglia and Germany. The flight is currently passing through a transitional period, exchanging its traditional wooden-hulled craft for larger steel-hulled vessels of greater endurance. 1967 saw the first of these, the 120 foot *HMAFV Seal*, a prototype craft capable of operating far out at sea on Search and Rescue duties or in support of maritime/air operations. The follow-up craft of this class, *HMAFVs Seagull* and *Sea Otter*, were commissioned at R.A.F. Mount Batten and underwent evaluation and acceptance trials under the auspices of the Squadron. Next to arrive for evaluation was *HMAFV Spitfire*, a 78-foot prototype steel-hulled replacement for the 68 foot Rescue/Target Towing Launch Mk 2, the much prized descendant of the wartime Air/Sea Rescue Launch. After lengthy trials and some modification, *HMAFV Spitfire* was accepted into service to be followed shortly afterwards by *HMAFVs Sunderland, Stirling* and *Halifax*. The present fleet at Mount Batten comprises *HMAFVs Sea Otter, Spitfire, Stirling, Halifax,* four of the older 63 foot wooden-hulled pinnaces and a 43 foot range *Safety Launch*, the wooden craft now being restricted to use in the ranges adjacent to Plymouth until they are replaced by more vessels of the Spitfire class.

Training Flight undertakes the basic training of recruits assigned to the marine trades of Motor Boat Crew and Marine Mechanic, and advanced training for personnel aspiring to become Coxswains, Master Coxswains and Marine Fitters. In addition, it provides familiarisation training for officers entering the Marine Branch and for telegraphists destined for employment in marine craft.

Engineering Squadron

This organisation is responsible for the overhaul and maintenance of all the marine craft at Mount Batten and for some aspects of maintenance on craft based at other stations as well. They fit and maintain all marine radio and radar equipment used in the various craft and ensure lifesaving equipment is kept up to standard. All the mechanical transport is run and repaired by the Squadron which also undertakes repairs and maintenance to most other machinery on the station.

In addition to these four areas of operations there are two other very important aspects of the role of R.A.F. Mount Batten today. The first is that the headquarters of the Southern Maritime Air Region is located here; this HQ forms an important part of Britain's maritime force and has responsibility for the safety of sea communications in the Atlantic and home waters. It is known as *SOUMAR* and works with *NORMAR*, a parallel organisation responsible for the northern areas around Britain. With the use of the long range maritime reconnaissance aircraft, the *Nimrods*, based in Cornwall, the Group has the peace time task of carrying out surveillance of potentially hostile surface vessels and submarines while maintaining standards adequate to ensure effective maritime operations in war. *SOUMARS'* area of interest extends from a line drawn between Ireland and the tip of Greenland down to the Tropic of Cancer. Both these organisations came about through the retitling of the former No. 19 Group at Mount Batten and No. 18 Group stationed near Edinburgh.

An air sea rescue demonstration from the Sound by helicopter showing the winch working.

Supply Squadron

This Squadron is located in the large building at the beginning of the Breakwater and has responsibilities for a supply control and accounting flight, a clothing store, accommodation stores, laundry, dry cleaning and a receipt and despatch section.

Administrative Squadron

This Squadron consists of Personnel Management Flight and Station Services Flight both located within the Station Headquarters. The first covers a wide range of responsibilities for personnel under the headings: Personnel Services, Accounts, Education, Continuation Training, Further Education at local Institutes, Resettlement, Station Library and Information Room. The second flight covers matters of accommodation, in the camp and at nearby married quarters, and medical services.

A helicopter about to land in front of the Officers' Mess.

The R.A.F. School of Combat Survival and Rescue is the second important area of responsibility being undertaken at R.A.F. Mount Batten. The position of the Station overlooking the Sound is ideal for this work and a comprehensive range of equipment, aids and craft are in constant use training many airmen personnel each year. The School was set up in 1943 and was moved to Mount Batten in 1959; in 1960 its work was extended to take in training for aircrew for escape, evasion and conduct should they be captured in times of war.

The role of the School is to train aircrew of all ranks in the theory of sea and land survival and, where appropriate, with pracitcal exercises. The training of aircrew and physical education branch personnel for instructional duties also takes place on Dartmoor. Facilities are available for a limited number of Army Air Corps, Commonwealth and NATO aircrew as well as Government sponsored civilian aircrew to gain knowledge and experience.

A trials section of the unit is responsible for testing and evaluation of all survival equipment or aids which are new to the Service. Lastly the School provides instructors on a three month detachment basis for duties in other countries or in liaison with exercises. There are a variety of courses being run ranging from a few days duration to those of just over two weeks in length planned to give a wide range of knowledge and related experience in this important area of work.

Part of an exercise by personnel attending the School of Combat Survival and Rescue.

Famous Flights and People at Mount Batten

R.A.F. Mount Batten has probably had more important and distinguished civilian and military visitors, passing through or staying, than any other Station of a comparable size. This is due to its position in the far South-West and the role it played during the last war when it was the only link with the Middle East by plane and the first landing point for seaplanes coming across from America. Like the old town of Plymouth, this Station was a very important departure and receiving point for the many journeys across the Atlantic and down to the Mediterranean, a role that Plymouth has discharged for hundreds of years on the seas.

The first journey of note was the historic flight in 1919 of an American seaplane which was the first to successfully fly across the Atlantic landing at Lisbon and then, four days later, flying into Plymouth where it received a tumultuous reception. The plane, NC4, had a crew of six, piloted by Lt. Cdr. A. C. Read, U.S.N. He left Long Island on 27th May, 1919, with two other planes heading for the Azores some 1,350 miles away. Only one seaplane achieved the first stage of the flight, leaving a further 800 miles to be crossed by NC4 on its own. The original plan was for the three planes to fly together and, in the event of engine failure, the crew of any plane coming down could be rescued at once. The situation had changed dramatically and NC4 had no alternative but to fly alone if the undertaking was to be successful.

Lt. Cdr. Read left the Azores on 27th May, 1919, and headed for Lisbon which was reached after ten hours of flying. The crew rested for a few days then made the last stage to Plymouth landing in the Sound during the afternoon to welcoming crowds and photographers. The plane was towed to Mount Batten, hoisted out of the water and an official reception was later held by the R.A.F. and civic leaders on 7th June, 1919, including an address and short service of thanksgiving at the Mayflower Stone.

The early years of the development of seaplanes naturally resulted in quite a number of first crossings or long journeys being made by various crews operating from different stations in this country. Those flying out from Plymouth were particularly successful in pioneering routes to the Middle and Far East during the early 1920's and 1930's after the station had been reopened and developed as a seaplane base.

The Duke of Edinburgh being welcomed to the Station.

In 1928 a route was opened to Australia when four *Supermarine Napier Flying Boats* flew 16,500 miles under the command of Capt. Cave-Browne Cave. The Squadron left Plymouth Sound on 17th October, 1928, called at seventy ports on the way out and finally reached Melbourne without mishap to planes or crews. The purpose of the trip was to test out the new metal frames of the various aircraft under tropical conditions and then to call at different places while out there including the bases at Singapore and Hong Kong. Although this journey may now appear not to be all that significant, it must be borne in mind that the seaplanes only had a maximum speed of only 108 m.p.h., the crews had to live in the planes and much of the route was largely uncharted. The effect, if any, of tropical storms on the metal planes was not then known.

Another "first" for the station came in 1930 when the longest formation trip for seaplanes set out for Iceland to join millenary celebrations in that country under the Icelandic Government. Six years later in 1936 the appropriately named *Singapore Flying Boat* set out from Mount Batten for Singapore on the first journey of its kind across India where tropical and monsoon conditions were encountered and the plane subjected to stringent flying conditions. The later stages of this flight were very difficult as supplies and fuel had to be man-handled out to the flying boat and the crew had to work under extremely difficult conditions.

The crew and seaplanes on their return from the 1928 Empire flight.

Senior officers and civilian personnel who passed through R.A.F. Mount Batten during the Second World War:

Alexander, Rt. Hon. A. V. First Lord Admiralty.
Auchinleck, General Sir Claude.
Bailie-Grohan, Rear Admiral, R.N.
Birdwood, The Lord, Field Marshal.
Brett, Major General, U.S. Army Air Service.
Bromet, G. R. Air Commodore.
Brooke-Popham, Sir Robert, Air Chief Marshal.
Charrington, H. Lieut. General.
Chatfield, The Lord. Admiral of the Fleet.
Coningham, A. Air Vice Marshal.
Cornwall, Sir John. Lieut. General.
Coryton, W. A. Air Commodore.
Cunningham, A. G. Lieut. General.
Dawson, W. L. Air Vice Marshal.
Dewing, R. H. Lieut. General.
Dill, Sir John, C.I.G.S.
Donovan, Colonel. U.S. Army, Official U.S. Observer.
Duff Cooper, Capt. the Rt. Hon. S. of S. for War.
Eden, Anthony the Rt. Hon. S. of S. for War.
Edgar, W. H. Surgeon Rear Admiral.
Evill, D. C. S. Air Vice Marshal.
Forbes, Sir Charles, Admiral of the Fleet.
Freeman, Sir William, Air Chief Marshal.
Fullard, P. Air Commodore.
Gairdner, Brigadier General.
Gardiner, G. H. Brigadier General.
Glennie, I. G. Vice Admiral.
Gloucester, Major General, the Duke of.
Gort, General, the Viscount.
Haining, Sir Robert, Lieut. General.
Halifax, R. H. C. Vice Admiral.
Harriman, Mr. Averill. Lease-Lend Representative.
Heywood, T. G. G. Major General.
Hopkins, Mr. Harry. Lease-Lend Representative.
Horton, Sir Max. Admiral of the Fleet.
Huddleston, Sir Hubert, Lieut. General.
Inglis, Brigadier General, N.Z.E.F.
Jackson, Sir Edgar and Lady Jackson.
Joubert de la Ferte, Sir Phillip, Air Chief Marshal.
Kent, Group Captain, the Duke of.
Klimecki, Lieut. General, Polish Army.
Lloyd, General Lord George.
Lloyd, H. P. Air Vice Marshal.
Lewis, Brigadier General.
Liddell, Sir Clive, Lieut. General.
Longmore, Sir Arthur, Air Chief Marshal.
Ludlow-Hewitt, Sir Edgar, Air Chief Marshal.
Lyster, A. L. St. G. Vice Admiral.
Lyttleton, Rt. Hon. Captain Oliver.
Maltby, P. C. Air Vice Marshal.
Martel, G le Q. Lieut. General.
Maynard, F. H. M. Air Vice Marshal.
McFarlane, Major General.
Moncton, Sir Walter, Minister of Information.
Musilier, Vice Admiral Free French Navy.
Nelson, Sir Frank Bart.
Payne, L. G. S. Air Commodore.
Percival, A. E. Major General.
Pope, V. V. Major General.
Pound, Sir Dudley. Admiral of the Fleet.
Pownall, H. R. Lieut. General.
Raikes, Sir Robert, Vice Admiral.
Reid, G. R. M. Air Vice Marshal.
Rice, Brigadier General.
Royce, Lieut. General, U.S. Army.
Sandford, Brigadier General.
Selessie, Hailie, Emperor of Abyssinia.
Shearer, Brigadier General.
Sikorski, Generalissimo, Polish Army.
Simpson, S. P. Air Commodore.
Slatter, L. H. Air Commodore.
Smith, A. F. Lieut. General.
Somerville, Sir James. Vice Admiral.
Stevenson, D. F. Air Commodore.
Stokes, R. S. G. Brigadier General.
Sturgess, Major General.
Tavener, R. L. Brigadier General.
Tedder, A. W. Air Marshal.
Tovey, Sir John, Admiral of the Fleet.
Van de Spuy, K. R. Lieut. General.
Wallerby, Brigadier General.
Walsh, Air Commodore, R.C.A.F.
Wavell, Sir Archibald, General.
West, Brigadier General.
Whitcombe, Brigadier General.
Whitley, Brigadier General.
Williams, Sir Guy, Lieut. General.

The following people have inspected the Station during the past thirty years:

The Rt. Hon. Winston Churchill
The Rt. Hon. Mr. Menzies
Admiral of the Fleet, Sir Charles Forbes
Admiral of the Fleet, Sir Martin Dunbar Nasmith
Marshall of the R.A.F. Viscount Trenchard
Air Chief Marshal Sir Ludlow-Hewitt
Air Chief Marshal Sir Frederick Bowhill
Air Chief Marshal Sir William Mitchell
Air Marshal Sir Leslie Gossage
Major General W. Green
Major General C. W. Alfrey
Air Vice Marshal F. G. D. Hards
Air Commodore J. A. Chamier
Group Captain the Duke of Kent
H.R.H. Duke of Edinburgh
H.R.H. Queen Elizabeth the Queen Mother

Commanding Officers at R.A.F. Mount Batten:
Wg. Cdr. S. W. Smith, O.B.E. 15.1.1929
Wg. Cdr. J. P. Burling, D.S.C., D.F.C., A.F.C. 1.10.1931
Wg. Cdr. J. O. Andrews, D.S.O., M.C. 31.12.1932
Gp. Capt. I. T. Lloyd 21.2.1934
Wg. Cdr. J. A. Sadler 7.6.1935
Gp. Capt. P. E. Maitland, M.V.O., A.F.C. 20.1.1936
Wg. Cdr. K. B. Lloyd, A.F.C. 5.2.1937
Gp. Capt. E. Digby Johnson, A.F.C. 19.10.1937
Gp. Capt. H. W. Evans 15.12.1939
Gp. Capt. L. Martin, A.F.C. 8.1.1942
Gp. Capt. J. Alexander, O.B.E., R.A.A.F. 1.4.1943
Gp. Capt. W. S. Caster, M.C. 7.11.1944
Sqn. Ldr. W. M. Lloyd 1.2.1946
Wg. Cdr. L. R. Flower, M.B.E., M.M. 1.4.1961
Wg. Cdr. D. T. Beamish, O.B.E. 23.3.1964
Wg. Cdr. E. N. Stone, M.B.E. 30.9.1966
Wg. Cdr. P. Wevill 4.4.1969
Wg. Cdr. K. P. Lucas 28.9.1970
Wg. Cdr. J. N. Burgess 14.8.1972
Wg. Cdr. A. Redfern 28.8.1974
Wg. Cdr. J. E. F. Williams 22.10.1976
Wg. Cdr. J. S. Fosh 9.2.1979

The Meteorological Office

The Meteorological Office at Mount Batten is the oldest unit on the station and has been in continuous operation since 20th August, 1920. It is now situated in a single-storied building on the higher ground to the left of the main road next to the Station Headquarters. Although this office, like many others, is within the service station, it is staffed by civilians and comes under the control of the Ministry of Defence. A prime function of the office is to fulfil the requirements of R.A.F. units in the area.

The extent and importance of its work, in co-operation with other regional offices and the main meteorological office at Bracknell, has developed over the years to a point where its early forecasters would probably be astonished now at the number of calls it receives each year and the volume and frequency of information it supplies to military and civilian organisations and individuals. With the development of complex information receiving and despatch apparatus and now the introduction of visual display units, information retrieval systems, including print-out pictures transmitted from satellites, the most up-to-date weather details can be made available to many people either through the post office, television, radio or by direct phone.

The office itself has been accommodated in a variety of buildings at Mount Batten and, during its early days, was not working on a round-the-clock basis and was dependent on relatively simple apparatus. Indeed, before the last war the office was manned by just two civilians; in 1926 it had a total of 187 enquiries during that year and in the 1930s this went up to about 300 per year. In 1937 a teleprinter unit was installed replacing wireless telegraphy as the main communication system. As was to be expected the war seriously hampered its work on a number of occasions but it also made new demands for weather information when the Sunderland Flying Boats were called out for rescue or patrol work. It was, in fact, the war that highlighted the importance of accurate weather forecasting and the need to keep an up-to-the-minute check on the ever changing patterns of weather both over land and sea. There was also considerable liaison between the various services in the Plymouth area especially during the build up for the Normandy Landings in 1944. During the immediate post-war years the met. office was relegated to an observing office and was transferred for a short period to Mount Wise together with other units from this station. A new role, however, was undertaken after 1948 when it was decided to make available weather information to civilian individuals and organisations. Little was it then realised that this side of the work would considerably increase to a point where thousands of calls come in each year from almost every section of the community from farmers to sailing enthusiasts, to schools and people asking about weather conditions for walking on Dartmoor.

In addition to its R.A.F. and other service requirements, this office now supplies weather data to all the radio, television and other media outlets and to the Post Office. The widespread growth in leisure activities, especially those connected with the sea, has resulted in almost an explosion of requests for prevailing weather conditions and, to give an example, there were over one million calls in the South-West region for the G.P.O. recorded forecast service in the year 1978.

The main work of this office can be broadly treated under two headings. The first covers the collection and transmission to headquarters of weather reports coming into the office from numerous places and people throughout the South-West. These range from coastguards, airfields, private individuals who have shown an interest in weather, water authorities, from Mount Batten itself and from many others, using instruments provided by the Meteorological Office.

One of the many daily readings being made at the "Met. Office".

The other role of this office is to give out to local regional and national outlets weather forecasts for the South-West region and the surrounding sea areas. This information can then be sent out through the media or made use of by the other regional offices or in the compilation of forecasts for aviation use. To fulfil its forecasting role a vast amount of information is necessary and data also comes in from other regional offices, airports, other countries and from the main meteorological office at Bracknell near London. The introduction of weather satellites has given a new dimension to this work and weather pictures are automatically printed out showing the cloud patterns prevailing over different parts of the planet. The use of very sophisticated electronic communication systems has brought to regional offices all this necessary information together with the output from the vast computer at Bracknell, so enabling more accurate and reliable weather forecasts to be made.

Perhaps the most direct and appreciative understanding of the office's work is during times of very bad weather or when there are heavy falls of snow or rain when lives are at risk or animals or livelihoods are placed in jeopardy.

R.A.F. MEMORIAL WINDOW

This very fine stained glass window in the Officers' Mess was rededicated in 1958 having been moved from R.A.F. Pembroke Dock Flying Boat Base following the Station's closure. The window depicts two Air Force officers looking out to sea with an aircraft overhead and an air sea rescue launch making for harbour. It also incorporates crests of the Australian and American Air Forces, the first having played a very important role during the last war both at Pembroke Dock and Mount Batten.

The memorial was first installed in the small church at Pembroke Dock Station and it was appropriate that its unveiling here was undertaken by the last Commander of that Station, Group Capt. P. A. Lombard. The window is best viewed in the early part of the day when the sun brings into prominence the colouring and detail in the stained glass.

ROLL OF HONOUR, St. John's Church

Two Rolls of Honour listing personnel who died during the Second World War at the Station are in the nearby church of St. John, Hooe. They commemorate those who died both from the Royal Air Force and the Royal Australian Air Force and on Remembrance Day each year a service is held in the church and wreaths laid on the altar. The photograph shows one of these services with the wreaths held by serving men taking place following the parade from the Station to the church.

OFFICERS of No. 238 SQUADRON

This very rare photograph shows the serving officers of No. 238 Squadron, R.A.F. Cattewater, which was taken in 1928. Seated left to right: Dr. W. E. M. Corbett, Flt. Lt. G. E. Livcock, D.F.C., Sqdn. Ldr. G. F. Breese, D.S.C., Flt. Lt. N. B. Ward, Flying Officer F. C. B. Saville. Top row: Sgt. Major J. C. Hallett, Flying Officers H. P. Strong, J. Stevens and A. S. Berry. Obsr. Officer W. McGowan, Sgt. Major M. R. Johnstone.

OFFICERS' MESS

The Officers' Mess is shown to good effect in this aerial photograph of the higher land of the Station backed by the very busy Cattewater. This once quiet estuary, where the river Plym enters the sea, has almost all of its banks built upon and much of its area is now used for safe anchorage for small ships and yachts. The open green land of the Station forms a pleasant contrast to the built-up areas of Turnchapel, Hooe and Oreston and provides one of the best areas overlooking the Sound.

MOUNT BATTEN BREAKWATER

This unusual photograph of the long breakwater running out from the headland and Station gives a good idea of the effect it can have on rough seas. The estuary and sheltered water behind it gave safe anchorage to many sailing ships seeking shelter and also, to pilots bringing in seaplanes, a recognisable feature for carefully setting a descent course before reaching the water. The smaller seaplanes in use here were lifted from the sea by a crane and kept on the breakwater.

EMPIRE AIR DAY

PUBLIC TO BE ADMITTED TO BATTEN AIR STATION

AN AFTERNOON OF THRILLS

THE ROYAL AIR FORCE ARE GOOD weather prophets, but Empire Air Day, which takes place to-day has presented them with a more difficult "forecast."

The Mount Batten station is being open to the public for the first time, and in the absence of reliable data, the Chairman of the Air Day Committee, has been wondering how many visitors to expect.

"We don't know whether to prepare for 500 or 5,000," said the chairman (Flight Lieutenant V. P. Feather) to our representative.

From Fairey to Perth

The attractions of the first Air Day— a sort of Cattewater "Navy Week" compressed into a single afternoon—will, however, be such as to draw a large "gate." Forty air stations in Britain will be holding similar "at homes," and the public are invited to watch workshop activities of the station, the evolutions of the machines, from the fragile Fairey to the giant Perth, and inspect the various branches of technical work, —the ground jobs which are necessary to keep the flying man in the air.

Certain "secrets" will be kept locked up, but the main work of the station on a busy day will be on view.

It may be possible for visitors who desire the experience to venture into a poison gas chamber, equipped, of course, with a Service gas-mask. This "attraction" has not been definitely settled, but in any case members of the R.A.F. personnel will give demonstrations in the gas chamber, part of their ordinary training.

Wireless Signals

Another interesting "exhibit" will be a portable wireless transmitter, similar to those used in the Iraqui desert, by which visitors will be permitted to signal instructions to machines in the air (although, of course, it will be useless to signal a Perth pilot to loop the loop!) The public will be allowed to make a close inspection of the various aircraft, but not to go on board. The objection is that the confined space would make a procession of sightseers a tedious business—much worse even than the tortuous progress through a submarine in Navy Week—and there is one instance in R.A.F. annals in which a stout lady got stuck in the entrance to the saloon!

In the workshops you may find out what a 100 miles an hour "breeze" feels like when a 550 h.p. Napier engine is being tuned up, or you may wander into the photographic section and see the marvels of the F 24.

Arthur L. Clamp – the man behind the books

Arthur Leslie Clamp was a man of boundless energy with a passion for helping others, particularly through his love of history. A printer by trade, he started his career in a printing company before moving his family from Exeter to Plymouth to teach at the Plymouth College of Art and Design, where he eventually became the Head of the Printing Department.

Arthur with his five children.

A Devoted Family Man

Despite his love of teaching, Arthur prioritised his family, always making it home by 5:30pm for tea. He and his wife, Rosemary, raised five children: Susan, Angela, Elizabeth, David, and Steven. Arthur would often combine his love of family and history by taking his children on Sunday walks, encouraging them to appreciate historical monuments by taking photos or making crayon rubbings of gravestones for his books. The family home at 203 Elburton Road was a hub of activity, with a large garden, featuring a two-storey fort and a makeshift swimming pool.

A Lifelong Learner and Adventurer

Arthur's thirst for knowledge extended beyond history to a deep curiosity about the world. He was passionate about exploring different cultures, traditions, and cuisines, often taking advantage of his long summer holidays as a teacher to travel to places like India, Russia, South America, the middle east and the USA, sometimes bringing one of his children along. This adventurous spirit even influenced his home life, as seen by the short-lived family tradition of steam-cooking vegetables after a trip to Iceland.

History is a prominent feature of family days out

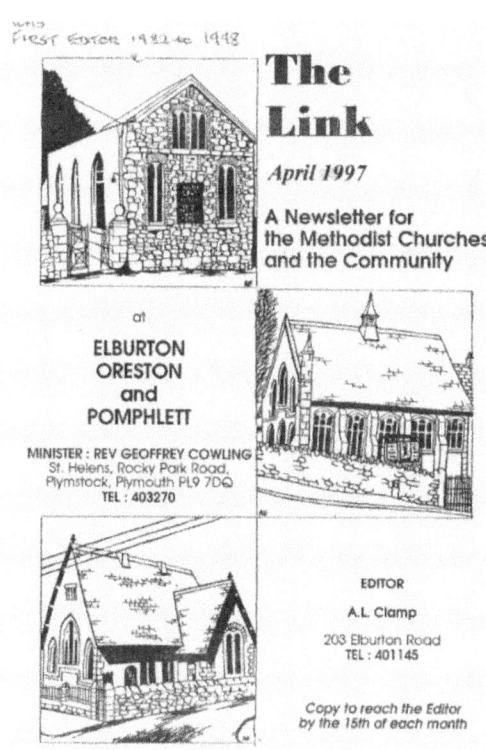

Community and Philanthropic Spirit

His commitment to serving others was evident in his long-standing involvement with the Elburton Methodist Church. He was the Sunday School Superintendent for over 15 years and served as the editor of the wider church's monthly newsletter, "The Link," for a similar duration. After Rosemary's very sad passing, Arthur later remarried and, following a chance encounter with a professor from India, established a connection with a missionary school in Chennai. Together with his new wife, Christine, he co-founded a "Sponsor a Child's Education" program that continues to this day.

Pictured left – The cover of 'The Link' complete with hand drawn sketches of each church by Angela
Below right – Arthur Clamp promoting his latest book
Below left – Arthur at home with his first wife, Rosemary
Below centre – Arthur on holiday with his second wife, Christine

A Legacy of Learning and Positivity

Arthur's greatest passion was history, which he brought to life through tireless research, documentation, and the many books he authored. He was driven by a need to "never be stuck in a rut," constantly seeking new experiences, meeting new people, and expanding his knowledge. With a positive attitude and a great sense of humour, he was always ready to help others, leaving a lasting impact on his family and community. His children, Susan, Angela, Elizabeth, David, and Steven, remember him with love and gratitude.

David Clamp, 2025

A Legacy of Local History

Below is the story of how Arthur L Clamp began writing books, in his own words, drafted shortly before he passed away in 2001. I have only made minor alterations to this text, correcting grammatical errors that he did not survive to correct himself. When I first discovered this text, I was shocked to see my name mentioned. It seems that, unbeknownst to me, I shared my first PC with him. I suspect he used it during the day when I was at school, although I do have one memory of sitting with him and showing him how it worked. It has been a pleasure to pick up where he left off and see his books republished and redistributed, and to know that I was part of the story, even back then. It was also fascinating to discover that his pricing structure matches the way I have tried to price the books, with a third going to local sellers and the rest covering printing costs with a little left over for my expenses.

I am his eldest grandson, and it is a privilege to curate his legacy, which we are calling 'The Clamp Collection'. The very last line of the text originally reads "The following pages list all the titles." Sadly, that page is missing and we have no record of all the books he published and knowing that some of those were researched by other authors makes the process of finding them even harder. I look forward to one day completing the collection and seeing them all available again. And maybe, one day, I'll even start writing my own to add to the series. For now, here is his story in his own words.

Steven Gibson, 2025

Writing and Publishing Booklets on Local Topics and Areas

I started this interest in either 1968 or 1969 when living in Woodford. I had by these dates established the Department of Printing and I think I must have been looking for something different to do. The first titles were of A5 size proofed from type set at Clarke, Doble and Brendon, Ltd., Plymouth printers, and then made up into pages and printed at Sawtell and Neilson, Ltd., Totnes.

Then began a slow process of getting them out to shops, etc. which proved to be more time consuming and difficult than actually researching, writing and getting the books into print. However, I persisted and opened a business account with Barclays Bank on the Broadway. I was advised to give it a title so I called it "Westway Publications". There came along another problem, one of storage of paper and finished books which was solved when the family moved to Elburton in 1970.

I changed the printer to Penwell, Ltd., Callington, Cornwall, as he was then just setting up himself and his prices seemed very reasonable. I did not get any of the printers to make up the complete books. I hand folded the flat printed sheets, stitched the books on a small manual table stitcher and trimmed them in a small hand turned guillotine which I bought from someone in Penzance for £40. It was brought up in a van.

The trouble and time going to and fro to Callington was too much so I transferred the printing to PDS Printers, Prince Rock, Plymouth, and I have been with them ever since. Now they are at Plympton which is easy to reach and they fold the flat sheets which was turning out to be a long chore which only saved a small part of the printing costs.

All my first titles were written by myself. I took the photographs and developed them in the loft of the house, the type was set by now on a computer situated in the house at Elburton from which I had collected photographic lengths of text to cut up and law down as pages.

At some point I decided that I would do my own film processing of lith film so I bought a large second hand process camera from Kingsbridge and learnt through trial and error to make line negatives of the text and halftone negatives of the illustrations which proved more difficult than I anticipated. The main problem was trying to keep the developer in the large dish at the correct temperature as any change would affect the developing time. I replaced this old camera with a brand new one bought from Croydon, Surrey, costing £900. This has turned out to be a great asset cutting out an expensive part of the printer's costs and one crucial aspect of the work which I could control.

By the middle 1970s there were many outlets I had contacted in Plymouth, up to Dartmoor, Exeter, around to Torbay, Totnes, Dartmouth and the South Hams. The market for local books was much greater than I had first thought and through getting to know many local people undertaking research themselves had the chance to help and make up books for other people who had in most instances, got together a collection of photographs with some text in a rather muddled way. Through my experience in print I was able to shape up their work and get it into print and in every case I had to pay the printer and let the person have the royalties. In the majority of titles produced in this manner this was another way of producing titles and it did give some profit to my work. However, I must say that in a few cases I lost out by either the other person getting the numbers wrong, not returning any monies from stock I delivered or they thought that more of their books should have been sold.

The print run was usually 1,000 copies and from time to time I have had reprints of 250 copies. It took about ten years to clear the first print run so I always had large stocks in the garage, workshop, etc. The numbers sold during the early years was about 7,000 copies a year increasing to around 9,000 copies and for the whole of the enterprise about 500,000 have been sold. The booklets have become part of the local scene and many people collect them, shops regularly order copies and I go around certain areas month by month restocking or replacing titles as necessary.

During the past year or so I have started setting the text on a Packard Bell PC, something which I should have done some years back. I share it with Steven Gibson, my grandson. There appears to be no end to the market for local books, but I could not earn a regular income because of the long time it takes to sell stock.

However, now exceeding 100 titles made up mainly of A4 twenty-four page booklets, some folded guides, with selling prices set with a third going to the shop which is the trade custom, the original idea has been quite successful and could go on for ever.

Apart from monetary benefits, however spasmodically these might be, I have learnt a lot myself, met many interesting people and have become part of the local scene with requests to give talks and to advise people about getting into print.

Arthur L Clamp, 2001

Death of local historical author

'He was an incredible character who was just loved by everybody who knew him'

A WELL-loved Elburton author has died at the age of 68.

Arthur Clamp (pictured right), who was one of the West Country's most successful writers, died at St Luke's Hospice, Turnchapel, after losing his battle against cancer.

Tributes have been flooding in for a man who was known in the community as a prominent writer and outgoing person.

He produced more than 140 titles during his life, dealing with both fiction, fact and history, often discussing West Country topics that were close to his heart.

One of his most acclaimed books was *The Plymouth Blitz*, and he also won credit for *The Rise and Fall of the Bearings of Membland Hall*, set in Noss Mayo.

He achieved sales of between 7,000 and 9,000 books every year and it is estimated that he has sold over half a million books, covering the areas of Plymouth, Dartmoor, Exeter, Torbay and the South Hams.

Mr Clamp was born in Mitcham, Surrey, in 1932, and was the eldest of four children.

He moved to Devon in 1941 to avoid the London air-raids.

Mr Clamp trained as a printer in Exeter and also gained a teachers' certificate in 1959 from Garnet College in London.

Plymouth College of Art, however, was to prove to be Mr Clamp's working home for the following 32 years until 1991, when he retired as head of the printing department.

He had a great interest in travel and had visited the USA, Tanzania, China, Russia, Peru, as well as travelling across Europe, where he presented talks and slide shows on his experiences as a writer.

Mr Clamp was a member of Elburton Methodist Church for many years, superintendent of the Sunday school and editor of the church newsletter, as well as being involved in much charity work.

He was president of the Plymouth and District Field Club and an active member of the Elburton Residents' Association.

He enjoyed leading walks on Dartmoor and historical tours throughout the West Country.

Mr Clamp married his first wife, Rosemary, in 1956 and they had five children– Susan, Angela, Elizabeth, David and Steven – and she died in 1987. He also had 11 grandchildren.

He leaves a wife Christine, after remarrying in 1991, and her two children and three grandchildren.

'He was an incredible character who was just loved by everybody who knew him,' said his wife.

'He will be missed by his family, his friends, the people he worked with and just everybody who knew him through his books.'

More than 300 mourners attended his funeral at Elburton Methodist Church on Monday.

The attendance was a celebration of his life – he would have found that really special. It shows his vibrancy and love of people,' said Mrs Clamp.

Steven Clamp added that his father was 'a well respected and loved man, missed by a great many people throughout the South West and far beyond'.

This newspaper article, published by the Evening Herald on 17th August 2001, forms a good record of his life. Just as he encourages us to learn more about local history, we encourage you to learn a little about him. For that reason, we have included these pages at the back of all the most recently republished books, in honour of his memory and recognition of his contribution to the community.

www.ingramcontent.com/pod-product-compliance
Lightning Source LLC
Chambersburg PA
CBHW061409070526
44584CB00031B/4195